VIOLENCE IN SCHOOLS

The Enabling Factor

Carole Remboldt

JOHNSON INSTITUTE

HAZELDEN®

Acknowledgment

The content of this booklet is based on the violence intervention and prevention model originally developed by Carole Remboldt for the Johnson Institute.

Violence in Schools: The Enabling Factor

Copyright © 1994 Hazelden Foundation. Previously published 1994 Johnson Institute-QVS, Inc. First published by Hazelden 1998. All rights reserved. No part of this book may be reproduced or transmitted in any form or by any means, electronic or mechanical, including photocopying, recording, or by any information storage and retrieval system, without express written permission from the publisher.

Hazelden Information and Educational Services
Center City, Minnesota 55012-0176
1-800-328-9000 (Toll Free U.S., Canada, and the Virgin Islands)
1-651-213-4000 (Outside the U.S. and Canada)
1-651-213-4590 (24 hour Fax)
www.hazelden.org

ISBN 1-56246-096-X

Cover and page design: Daniel Crombie
Printed in the United States of America

Table of Contents

Introduction

Every day it's in the news: A child is shot on school grounds. Another is seriously injured by a bully. A teacher is assaulted. Gangs coerce students to join them or pay the price. A local high school installs metal detectors. A local middle school hires an armed security guard to patrol the halls. Violence and fear of violence are very real problems in today's schools.

Eradicating weapons and gangs from a school once they are there can be an overwhelming, if not nearly impossible, task. But long before weapons enter the building or gangs begin recruiting, violence is happening in our schools. It happens on the playground where the first graders play. It happens in the lunchroom where the fourth graders eat. It happens in the hallways where the seventh and eighth graders move from class to class. And it happens in the high school classroom where students are trying to learn.

How pervasive is the problem of violence in our schools? While some data derived from national surveys indicate the problem is widespread and growing rapidly, an exact measure of the degree of violence present in today's schools is not yet available. Many incidents of violence go unreported or are underreported. The students or staff who are victims of the violence either don't report it or those to whom they report it often fail to document the incidents in a meaningful way. And they often fail to do anything about it. A Louis Harris survey of students and teachers found that nearly one in four students and one in ten teachers say they have been victims of violence on or near school property.

The most commonly reported incidents involved pushing, shoving, grabbing, hitting, verbal insults and threats, and stealing.[1]

Of course, these aren't the types of events that make the news. Yet it's these kinds of hostile interactions among students and between students and teachers that are indeed the most common and that often lead up to the violent incidents we hear about in the news.

Even though 25 percent of big city public schools have installed metal detectors, school violence is not just an urban problem. A 1993 National School Boards Association survey found that 43 percent of rural school administrators reported increased violence in their schools, compared with five years earlier.[2] Eugene Wheeler and S. Anthony Baron, Ph.D., in their book, *Violence in Our Schools, Hospitals and Public Places*, cite a 1990 study conducted by Texas A&M University.[3] The university concluded that "many rural public schools, especially those near large cities, have worse violence problems than the national average." Texas A&M surveyed 1,004 eighth and tenth graders from 23 small communities in central Texas. The following were among the findings cited by Wheeler and Baron:

- 34 percent of students reported having been threatened with bodily harm at school or on a school bus.

- 15 percent claimed they had something taken from them by force or threat of bodily harm.

- 14 percent said they had been physically attacked and 6 percent admitted that someone tried to force them to have sex.

- Half the boys and 28 percent of the girls were in at least one fight during the previous year.

- Students believed they should fight if someone: hit them (78 percent); hurt someone they care about (74 percent); insulted their family (58 percent); or purposefully broke something they own (53 percent).

- More than 20 percent said that threatening to use a weapon would help prevent fights.

- Nearly 17 percent thought "acting tough" would deter altercations.

Johnson Institute's *StudentView*® Surveys indicate that a fairly well-defined group of students are involved repeatedly in starting physical fights or beating people up. Slightly over 4 percent of girls and nearly 14 percent of boys are involved in beating people up or starting physical fights three or more times a year. Girls' involvement in violence at school, however, is probably underrepresented by this data because girls tend to use less physical means of violence, such as verbal attacks or social exclusion.

Regardless of who is committing the violent acts, boys or girls, or whether the problem is greater in the cities, suburbs, or small towns and rural areas, addressing violence problems day in and day out is not what most educators bargained for when they chose their careers. Most teachers, administrators, school counselors, and other professionals working in education chose their professions because they had a burning desire to make a difference in children's lives—to spread knowledge and make the world a better place by guiding and instructing young minds. Those aspirations are too often shot down when educators work in school environments where violence against students and teachers is all too common. Many feel overwhelmed by hopelessness and helplessness. They feel powerless to do anything to make the school a safe, supportive, and nurturing place for learning. They fear confronting students about their violent behavior because they don't feel adequately equipped to intervene effectively. Many feel nothing will be done about violent student behavior even if they do report it. Others believe incidents of violence may be handled poorly or perhaps in an overly punitive way. And yet others simply resent that so much of their workday is spent *disciplining* children instead of *teaching* them. Schools that have already attempted to implement single-focus or piecemeal strategies to combat violence problems, such as installing metal detectors, hiring guards, searching lockers and other "get tough" approaches, have met with little, if any, success.

So, what can schools do? This booklet doesn't pretend to have any complete answer because violence in schools is a difficult and multifaceted problem. It is, in fact, a *systemic* problem that will require a systematic approach to solve.* Much has been written about the causes of violence in our society. However, specifically concerning violence in schools, Johnson Institute has identified some major factors that appear to stand out:

- *Disinhibition of children toward violence.* We live in an increasingly violent society where violent behavior is often depicted as glamorous, exciting, and the pathway to power. Between media images and real-life examples of peers using violence to their advantage at home, at

---

* The Johnson Institute has developed the *Respect and Protect* Program, a systematic approach for solving violence problems in schools. To learn more, read: *Solving Violence Problems in Your School: Why a Systematic Approach is Necessary* (Minneapolis: Johnson Institute, 1994).

school, and on the streets with only minimal consequences imposed by adults, it's not surprising that many children have become disinhibited to violent behavior. This disinhibition has created a serious problem for schools and placed enormous pressure on educators to do something to solve the problem.

• *Lack of a clear and universally accepted definition of violence.* Violent behavior in an individual child rarely starts suddenly with the *big* things, such as shooting, fighting, stabbing, or vandalizing. Long before these things occur, there are the "little things": mean or hurtful words, looks, signs, gestures, and covert acts, such as silent threats and social isolation. Teasing, name calling, a flip of a finger, a demeaning facial expression, however, too often lead to a push, a shove, a hit, a punch, a fight . . . someone pulling out a weapon. But by many standards and definitions used in schools—and society as a whole—only the physical actions count when it comes to defining violence.

A simple working definition of violence for educators, that is used in the Johnson Institute's *Respect and Protect* program and that encompasses these nonphysical but equally hurtful acts, is:

> *Violence occurs whenever anyone inflicts or threatens to inflict physical or emotional injury or discomfort upon another person's body, feelings, or possessions.*

Translated for children and adolescents, the definition is:

Violence is any mean word, look, sign or act that hurts a person's body, feelings, or things.

- *Tolerance.* As Deborah Prothrow-Stith, M.D., assistant dean of the Harvard School of Public Health and an expert on teenage violence, points out in her book *Deadly Consequences: How Violence is Destroying Our Teenage Population*, "Teachers and school administrators often know what is going on, but feel powerless to halt the process leading up to a fight."[4] Similarly, Dan Olweus, Ph.D., who has studied bully/victim violence in Scandinavian schools for more than 20 years, found through his research that "teachers do . . . relatively little to put a stop to bullying at school, according to both the bullied and bullying students."[5] While there are certainly many instances in which teachers and other school professionals feel powerless to stop violent interactions among students, all too often they simply minimize the incidents—and the effect the incidents have on the victims—by writing them off as "something all children have to endure as part of growing up." But lack of action on the part of adults is perceived by children as *permission* to be violent. And this is what *tolerance of violence* is all about.

- *Entitlement.* The combination of children's disinhibition to violence and adults' tolerance of violence leads many students to think it's perfectly normal and acceptable to express their anger, get their needs met, or fulfill their desires through acts of violence. And if violence is perfectly normal and acceptable, there's no reason not to wield its power. Many children feel they have a right—they are, in fact, *entitled* —to use violence as they see fit.

- *Enabling.* Enabling is a form of counterproductive behavior that arises from our misguided beliefs, feelings, and attitudes about violence. Enabling, though unwitting, in the end makes it easier for school violence problems to develop and worsen because it prevents those who use violence from both realizing and experiencing the consequences of their actions. Again, enabling is unwitting, not intentional. Those who are enabling are unaware of its harmful effects. However, because entitlement and tolerance are really by-products of enabling and clearly fan the flames of student violence, we must address enabling if we are to effectively eliminate entitlement and tolerance from the school setting.

Until now, schools have done their best to curb the violence, but too often their efforts have had only limited effect because they have focused primarily on what amounts to be only one or two facets of a multifaceted problem. Installing metal detectors, hiring armed security guards or police officers, searching lockers, placing cameras on buses, and other attempts to counteract violence are all well-intentioned, but piecemeal attempts at preventing violence. Often they serve only to drive the problem underground, leaving students and teachers more vulnerable after school or outside school grounds. "Get tough" measures designed primarily to ensure that weapons are not present fail to address the real underlying causes of violence in schools. They fail to teach children empathy and respect for others or the skills of anger management and conflict resolution.

Before any further attempts at solving violence problems in their schools can be effective, educators must first be willing to look at enabling. They need to identify the ways in which they may unwittingly be enabling the escalation of violence problems in schools. The pervasive attitudes of entitlement and tolerance are really the result of an "enabling system"—that is, systemwide enabling by administrators, teachers and other staff, parents, and students themselves.

What exactly *is* an enabling system and how does it manifest itself in schools? Answering that question for those who are concerned about student violence problems is the purpose of this booklet. For only when we understand that entire *enabling system* and set about dismantling it, can we even begin to solve violence problems in schools. The experiences of schools across the country bear witness that no single person or single-facet policy, program, or strategy, on its own, has a chance of cracking the multifaceted problem of violence in our schools.

The Concept of Enabling

Before describing exactly what an enabling system is, we should be very clear on two important points.

- With regard to attempts to solve a systemic problem such as violence, the term "enabling" is by no means positive, as it is in many other contexts ("His financial expertise *enabled* him to solve the company's debt problems."). Why? Because enablers are enabling a harmful situation (student violence) to continue and even grow worse.

- On the other hand, that doesn't in any way mean that those who are part of the enabling system have *caused* the problems or that they should *blame themselves* for their part in it. Why? Because enabling behaviors that help to spawn and sustain violence problems are *unwitting*, not *deliberate* or *intentional*, as we'll see later. We shouldn't feel guilty about what we've done unwittingly or unintentionally.

An enabling system is comprised of all the misguided beliefs, feelings, attitudes and behaviors that unwittingly allow and encourage student violence problems to continue or worsen by preventing those who engage in violence from understanding and experiencing the consequences of their behavior.

Note that in this definition, enabling isn't just a matter of the enablers' misguided behaviors: the definition recognizes that the enablers' misguided *beliefs, feelings,* and *attitudes* concerning violence *also* contribute to the elaborate system of enabling.

Misguided Beliefs, Feelings, Attitudes, and Behaviors Concerning Violence

Our misguided beliefs, feelings, attitudes, and behaviors concerning violence all contribute to the total school environment, an environment that spawns entitlement and tolerance and that enables violence problems to develop, continue, and worsen. All these elements make up the enabling system, and these elements lead to and reinforce one another so effectively that the enabling system is highly resistant to change. Thus, any attempt to dismantle the enabling system in the schools must address all these elements. Let's look at each one briefly.

Misguided Beliefs

Knowledge is power, and there is a significant cognitive aspect to enabling. Lacking accurate information about or a clear definition of violence, or believing in the many myths concerning the use of violence can aggravate violence problems and even help to foster and sustain such problems. Without a full awareness of the facts or of the complex nature and scope of violence, people are more likely to rely on simplistic reactions and "quick fixes" rather than on reflective and effective responses to violence. Some examples of overly simplified beliefs about violence include: "We wouldn't have a violence problem here if parents and the police would just do their jobs," or "Our problem isn't violence, it's not enough staff," or "We don't really need a violence program here on the elementary level, but the middle school surely does," or "It's not our job to do something about violence problems at school; that's the administration's responsibility."

Similarly, many educators, students, and parents believe they know who the "violent" kids are. Many believe that only gang members, "bad kids," or the kids who bring weapons to school are responsible for violence problems. As a result, schools install metal detectors or enact policies that are aimed at stopping the gang members, the bad kids, or kids who carry weapons. Unfortunately, these actions end up punishing everyone, while addressing only a small, though serious, part of the problem. Again, many people excuse (and therefore ultimately condone) a student's angry or violent interactions with peers or teachers with misguided assessments such as "He's just got a bad temper;" "He hit the teacher because he lost control;" "He didn't mean to do it; he's really a good kid;" or "She comes from a broken home and that's why she acts so mean;" or "I feel bad about those girls being harassed on the bus, but what can you do—boys will be boys." While all these things may be true about the students involved, they do not *justify* violent behaviors.

In the absence of a sound understanding and a clear definition of what constitutes violence, it's common for adults to regard violent behavior among students as a uniform phenomenon, springing from the same causes and cues. In this view, various kinds of student violence are seen as simply varying degrees of the same problem. What many are unaware of is that there are *qualitative* differences in the violent experiences of students, just as there are for adults. Strategies such as skills training in anger management and conflict resolution, while helpful for students when they are involved in normal kinds of conflict situations (arguments over relationships or possessions, who was first in line, who bumped into whom and so on), will be totally ineffective for students who are being abused by family members at home or repeatedly victimized by bullies at school. Moreover, information, counseling, and support group techniques that are helpful for victims of violence are ineffective for many perpetrators of violence unless combined with consequences. Some students are able to change their violent behavior by learning about how violence hurts their families, friends, classmates, and themselves (learning empathy) and by learning to manage anger and resolve conflicts nonviolently. For others, being made to pay the consequences of their behavior through a parent/school conference, reparation, lost privileges, or suspension may be enough to make them think twice before again acting violently. For still others, such as bullies, the involvement with violence may be so intense that a formal and highly structured intervention process, involving graduated levels of sanctions geared to the frequency and severity of the violent behavior, is needed before change can occur.*

Such a process may use a "no use of violence contract" for lesser or first time offenses, followed by more stringent contracts for more serious offenders. These would call for school and parental monitoring, mandatory participation in a predetermined level of support group, and restitution or legal action, if warranted. Violent behavior, however, can stem from something more than mere lack of empathy, skills for controlling anger or skills for resolving conflicts nonviolently. Some children and adolescents with serious or habitual involvement in violence may have character, personality, or conduct disorders. These students may be less likely to respond to *any* help the school offers through its structured intervention process and may need to be referred for psychological evaluation to a resource out-

---

* Johnson Institute's *Respect and Protect* Program for Solving Violence Problems in Schools contains such a formal and highly structured intervention element called Choices, Consequences, and Contracts. For more information, read *Solving Violence Problems in Your School: Why a Systematic Approach is Necessary*, (Minneapolis: Johnson Institute, 1994).

side the school. A psychological evaluation by a qualified professional may indeed show that for some of these students, placement in a long-term rehabilitation facility, an alternative school, or some other appropriate facility may be the only viable option if other students are to be safe. It is a common *misperception* that approaches aimed at resolving violence problems stemming from normal kinds of conflict are equally effective for resolving the problem of bullying behavior. The type of conflict that occurs between bullies and their victims is not related to normal disagreements, and it almost always involves violence. A bully chooses one or more victims and intentionally, repeatedly, and over time inflicts or threatens to inflict physical or emotional injury or discomfort. In addition to the repetitive pattern of violence, what makes bully/victim violence different from violence stemming from a student's inability to resolve conflicts nonviolently or to manage his or her anger is that bully/victim violence *involves an imbalance of power and strength*. It almost never involves conflicts or quarrels between two people of approximately the same size or physical or emotional strength. Furthermore, bullies are not interested in learning anger management or conflict resolution skills because bullies derive a certain pleasure and sense of power from what they are doing and are not interested in resolving disputes or handling their anger. Likewise, bully/victim situations are not amenable to nor can they be resolved through peer mediation.

It is critical that educators understand and provide effective responses to the problem of bully/victim violence. The dynamics of bully/victim violence are often misunderstood by educators and so the following misguided beliefs or myths about bullies and their victims are very common among educators and students:[6]

Myth: Most bullying takes place on the way to and from school so it's not the school's problem. In fact, most bullying takes place on the school grounds. Studies by Olweus[7] show that almost twice as many elementary students were bullied at school as on the way to and from school; for students in junior and senior high, bullying was three times more common at school than while en route.

Myth: The only reason bullying is a problem in schools is because classes are too crowded. While class size has not been shown to be a factor in bullying, "teacher density" on the playground and during free periods has. According to Olweus, "bullying and other unwanted behaviors occur when adults are not present or do not know what the children are doing."[8]

Myth: Bullying is an urban problem, often related to gangs. Bullying happens in urban, suburban, and rural schools alike. No school is bully-proof. Furthermore, gangs are not usually the problem. The type of violence spawned by gangs is usually between kids of perceived equal strength and happens for different reasons, such as power struggles, territorial transgressions, and others.

Myth: Bullying is a consequence of competition at school. Studies by Olweus show that both bullies and victims may tend to have lower grades. But there is no evidence that poor academic achievement is the cause of bullying.

Myth: Bullies are really anxious and insecure individuals who use bullying to hide their insecurities. Studies tend to indicate that bullies, as a group, are not any more anxious or insecure than other children, and are often less so. Furthermore, they do not usually suffer from low self-esteem. Bullies like to intimidate, threaten, dominate, and hurt others.

Myth: Bullies are usually the unpopular kids at school. While bullies may not be the most popular students, they usually have a close following of two to three other students. They rarely are among the least popular students in a school.

Myth: Bullies use violence on others because they have been victims of bullying themselves, either by adults or by stronger peers. While some bullies have at one time been victims of violence, by far the majority come from homes where the primary caretaker lacks emotional warmth and involvement, has been overly permissive about allowing aggressive behavior, is negligent about setting clear limits, and generally has permitted too much freedom and provided too little care.

Myth: Most bullying is done by boys. Although boys are more likely than girls to use physical violence and threats of physical violence, bullying by girls is common too, but is often more difficult to discover and so is underreported. Girl bullies typically use less visible and more *subtle* means of harassment such as slandering, spreading rumors, isolating others, and manipulating friendships (for example, depriving another girl of her best friend). Moreover, girls bully boys, as well as the other way around.

These and other misguided beliefs about violence problems in school need to be dispelled if educators are to stop enabling. Ignorance about violence can lead to misguided feelings, attitudes, and behaviors—three other components of the enabling system. If, for example, a teacher is unaware that a student lacks control over his or her violent behavior because of a conduct disorder or that the student is engaged in ongoing bullying of another child, that teacher is likely to use ineffective or even escalatory strategies, such as trying to mediate the current conflict through logic or imposing punitive consequences that lead the bully to retaliate against the victim. When the violent behavior continues, the teacher feels frustrated and inadequate, and whatever negative attitudes he or she may have brought to the situation about violence at school or the specific students involved will be reinforced. In the end, the student's violent behavior continues and perhaps progresses to more dangerous levels.

Similarly, many adults as well as students are not prepared for how cleverly bullies, in particular, can talk their way out of situations or difficulties when confronted about their behavior, recasting or outright lying about what really happened so it appears they did nothing wrong or even that it was the other student's fault. Without realizing this is the case, school professionals and peer mediators, in particular, are inclined to be taken in by the bully's story or rationalization. The bully's ability to rationalize the situation and even to sway others to his or her perspective, combined with the imbalance of power inherent in bully/victim relationships (the victim usually being physically or emotionally weaker and somewhat defenseless) creates a type of conflict that should never be referred to peer mediators for resolution. In fact, peer mediation may actually place the victim in further jeopardy. Bully/victim violence almost *always* requires *adult intervention*. But when adults are not informed about the dynamics of bully/victim violence,and believe that such incidents are a "natural part of growing up," or hold misguided beliefs about the role they should or should not play in such situations, they are likely to enable the bullying to continue. Ultimately, false ideas or lack of knowledge about enabling can make it impossible for us to identify and describe behavior that, in ourselves or in the system of which we are a part, is unwittingly allowing the violent behavior of students to continue.

Misguided Feelings

When we encounter students involved in violent incidents we almost always have an emotional reaction, perhaps anger, fear, disgust, concern, or some other feeling. If we are not careful, what we do with those feelings can contribute to the enabling system in subtle but powerful ways. How we identify and express those feelings to students and how students perceive our emotional reactions are far more important than the feelings themselves. For example, many teachers ask how they should respond when a student threatens them or another student in their classroom. They are usually surprised to learn that the most important thing they can convey to such students is how concerned they feel at such inappropriate behavior and how worried they are about what the students are doing to themselves and others. "When you threaten to use violence against me or one of your classmates, it really scares me. I'm very concerned about what you're doing now and about what will become of you. There are others ways for you to get your needs met and I'm willing to help you. But threatening people or using violence is *not* okay and I won't tolerate it."

Naturally a student cannot know our concerns unless we express them. Moreover, this expression of feeling, even if met with rejection ("Who cares how you feel and what you think?") can serve to defuse the situation and lets the student know that he or she has been heard and has other choices. It is very important for students to know our true feelings, including appropriate anger (when it is safe to express it) over their violent behavior. ("Corrina, I get angry when you use your power to threaten me or one of your classmates. I respect your strength, but not when you use it to hurt people. You have other choices for getting your needs met, but using violence is not acceptable and I won't tolerate it.").

If, however, our anger is heard as judgment, resentment, or blame ("You act pretty tough in here, but we'll see how tough you are when the principal gets hold of you."), the effect is to strengthen those defenses that block students' awareness of how inappropriate or unacceptable their behavior is and how it is affecting others. How we express our feelings has much to do with whether students make other choices about getting their needs met, or ask for help, or accept it when it is offered.

If we blame, judge, threaten, shame, or erode the students' self-esteem in other ways, our feelings will only strengthen students' unwillingness to change their behavior. Likewise, if we're unwilling, unable, or afraid to express our feelings, we will deprive students of important information about their behavior that they typically do not get from any other source. Thus, our own individual ego defenses and feelings (anger, resentment, hostility, hatred, disgust, vengefulness) can be part of the enabling system.

Misguided Attitudes

Our attitudes, especially stereotypes and judgmental attitudes about the type of students—both perpetrators and victims—who get involved in violent incidents, are another component of the enabling system.

Stereotypes are predispositions or ingrained habits of thinking or seeing. Inaccurate stereotypes such as "only the bad kids carry weapons" or "the (African-American, east side neighborhood, Asian, Hispanic, or any other group) kids start all the fights" or "the gangs are responsible for all the violence in this school" or "some kids are such geeks it's no wonder they get beaten up," often affect our vision and thereby contribute to our failure to recognize problems or their scope. Our stereotypes about the kinds of kids who are and are not involved in bringing weapons to school, in gang activity, or in starting fights or vandalizing property, narrow our vision. Preconceived notions about the "typical" perpetrators of violence or members of gangs can make it very difficult for us to identify and help the numbers of students who are involved in violent incidents, but who don't fit such stereotypes. The fact is, however, that most students who are involved in school violence problems don't conform to or fit those typical stereotypes. Instead, they are often average kids, boys and girls, scared or out of control, unfocused, lacking direction, looking for some kind of identity or for some way to protect themselves or stand out from the crowd.

Often inspired by racial prejudice, our judgmental attitudes about which kids are responsible for violence problems are frequently a component of the enabling system. Racially inspired judgmental attitudes are those that accuse, condemn, reject, blame, or otherwise threaten the personhood of students from various ethnic groups, especially those associated with lower economic or social status. Such attitudes often betray a desire to scapegoat, punish, or put-down those people whom we feel threatened by or superior to. Racially derogatory names carry profoundly negative connotations and label whole groups of people as "bad."

What we need to understand is that our stereotypical thinking and our judgmental attitudes have three significant consequences. First, they are *always expressed*—if not explicitly in words, then through our choice of facial expressions, signs, gestures, looks, tone of voice, or response to a given situation. Secondly, they are *always received*, because kids who feel inadequate or discriminated against are highly attuned to those in the environment who are communicating put-downs. Thirdly, our stereotyping and judgmental attitudes prevent those kids who need help from getting it. If a student (or group of students) senses that admitting involvement in violent incidents and accepting help to change his or her behavior means accepting that he or she is a "bad person," the student will not ask for the help, won't accept the help if it is offered, and if accepting the help is mandated, will sabotage it in some way. On the flip side, students who are involved in acts of violence, but don't fit the stereotype we've set, are more likely to be overlooked or not dealt with effectively.

Misguided Behaviors

We enable most visibly through the ways in which our misguided beliefs, feelings, and attitudes manifest themselves in our behavior—through things *we do* or *fail to do*. There are many acts of *commission* in this regard: ignoring, pretending not to see, excusing, covering up, or taking punitive action without thorough investigation or without first offering a student help to change, to name only a few. For example, many teachers, school counselors, and administrators will unwittingly condone or excuse students' threats of or actual violent behavior as "normal" adolescent behavior or as being understandable given the student's family background, home life, or the neighborhood he or she comes from. Some will fail to inform parents about students' violent behavior out of fear of parent reaction. Some coaches have been known to get players off the hook for violent behavior in order to protect their team's status and potential for winning games. Some principals suspend or expel students for violent behavior without first involving counselors or the staff of the Student Assistance Program who could look carefully at the violent situation or pattern of incidents to determine what help the student might need to change his or her behavior. More often than not, though, the enabling system in a school is characterized by what it fails to do—for instance, failing to recognize or actually denying violence problems, failing or refusing to talk openly about such problems, failing to intervene with or confront students engaged in violent behavior, or failing to enact policies that govern violent incidents or to enforce sanctions or consequences set forth by exiting policies. Many administrators are fearful of acknowledging the extent of violence problems for fear it might reflect negatively on the school's image in the community. Some schools may suspend or expel a student for violent behavior, only to rescind or reverse the decision when parents react strongly or threaten to go to the school board. Teachers often will ignore, rationalize, or refuse to report or refer a student for threats or actual violent behavior in a classroom out of fear of retaliation by the student or that student's friends, or for fear that the administration might decide the teacher lacks control over or cannot discipline unruly students, or more understandably, out of fear for his or her own immediate safety. Nevertheless, this "peace at any price" form of enabling only serves to compound the problem and does nothing to solve it. (More extensive lists of enabling behaviors that typify various roles in the schools are described later and in the checklists at the end of this booklet.)

So far, we have dealt with the components of the enabling system mostly as they promote or encourage violent behavior by students. But educators need to also examine problems of enabling that may affect staff behavior and further create an environment that allows violence to flourish and grow. For example, all staff members must be willing to thoroughly examine their own participation in violence by asking themselves such questions as these:

- Do we tolerate, rationalize, and thereby promote verbal or physical abuses of students by staff, rather than striving to develop healthy and respectful patterns of interactions with students?

- Do we fail to intervene with or confront staff members who do not appropriately manage their anger or control their tempers, or who use abusive or demeaning language or actions with students?

- Do we communicate through inaction that use of violence by staff is acceptable or warranted, thereby communicating to students the mixed message, "It's never okay to use violence . . . unless we're talking about us."?

- If a staff member is willing to deal with his or her anger management problem, will that person be supported or encouraged to get help, or will the person be punished in some way?

- Does the administration leave staff powerless to deal effectively with school violence problems by failing to adapt a clear and system wide school policy, as well as a strong school ethos of nonviolence that is collectively, consistently, and firmly enforced and communicated by all adults in the school?

How Enabling Functions

How does enabling function? The constellation of misguided beliefs, feelings, attitudes, and behavior allows violence problems to continue or worsen by preventing students from recognizing and experiencing the consequence of their violent behavior and by fostering the two pervasive attitudes of entitlement and tolerance—the fuel that inflames violence problems in schools. Students must be taught that the use of violence has consequences for themselves and for others. They need to be taught that violence hurts—their friends, their parents, their brothers and sisters, their classmates, their teachers, everyone. They need to understand that any mean word, look, sign, or act that hurts another person's body, feelings or possessions is violence and is totally unacceptable.

There are three ways to communicate to students the false message that the use of violence at school *does not* have consequences.

One way is to fail to lay down clear expectations of student behavior and consequences for all uses of violence in the school. A formal and highly structured intervention system that involves choices, consequences, and contracts and contains graduated levels of sanctions geared to the frequency and severity of students' violent behavior is ideal. If all the adults in a school do not consistently communicate and demonstrate that there are consequences for using violence (tolerance), then students are free to conclude that adults sanction the use of violence and therefore it is acceptable (entitlement).

A second way is to fail to enforce sanctions or consequences. When we do that, we deny students the opportunity to change their behavior and to learn to make healthy and appropriate decisions about the use of violence. Also, by having students know about consequences that aren't enforced, we contribute to the students lack of respect for us and the whole school system. By contrast, when students experience consequences or see their peers experience them (but without punitiveness), they learn which decisions to make, develop a sense of responsibility, and above all, feel safer and more secure in the school environment.

A third way is for all staff to fail to act in a collective, determined, and consistent way to demonstrate that they will not tolerate any form of violence in the school. A totally shared school ethos that communicates to students and adults, in effect, that "violence is not okay and we do not tolerate it here" is a very powerful prophylactic against violence. Ironically, this is not a militant, punitive ethos or empty threat. And it is communicated most powerfully through open and appropriate expression of feelings—of anger, fear, concern, even sadness whenever students use violence, whether through words, signs, looks, or acts that are hurtful to other persons' bodies, feelings, or possessions. The feelings that teachers or other staff experience as a result of students' use of violence are just as "factual" as the policies the students may violate.

When we fail in any of these ways to communicate to students the consequences of their use of violence, we're acting as enablers because we deprive students who use violence (as well as others in the school) of the information and experience they need if they are to realize that they must choose to stop their violent behavior, or that they may need help to do so.

Some Motives Behind Enabling

In domestic violence, family members, friends, neighbors, and even law enforcement agents who deny, cover up or make excuses for, or blame other people, places, circumstances or events for the perpetrators' abusive behavior are enabling the violence (even against themselves) to continue or worsen. In such families, members often actively take on the responsibility for the perpetrator's actions, defending the actions by rationalizing them ("Sometimes he hits us, but only when we've done something to make him mad.") or out of fear of reprisal if they don't defend them.

For example, Bill comes home late after a bad day at work. Fifteen minutes before quitting time, his boss confronted him about a project he hadn't yet finished. Although Bill is upset by his boss's implications that he isn't doing his job as well as he should, he stays and finishes the job, without calling home to say he will be late. Bill arrives home later that night in a foul mood. When his wife Gloria asks him if he would like her to heat up the dinner he missed earlier, he swears at her, calls her and the children insulting names and demands that they sit at the table while he eats. When the oldest child, Bill's 12-year-old stepson, says he can't come to the table because he has to study for a big test the next day, Bill walks over, yanks the boy out of his chair, yells at him and shoves him toward the kitchen table. When the boy pleads one more time that he has to study or he'll flunk his test, Bill begins to verbally and physically abuse him. His wife steps in, manages to get Bill off her son, then turns to her son and says, "Sammy, why can't you just do what he asks. Why do you always have to make him so mad. Please, just do what he asks."

Gloria tells Bill she really needs Sammy to walk to the convenience store to pick up milk for tomorrow's breakfast.

Bill tells Sammy to "get out of his sight" and do as his mother says. Gloria continues to placate Bill, brings his warm dinner to the table and changes the subject. They talk about how bad Bill's day was and Gloria reaffirms for Bill that his boss is a real jerk and Bill a good, hard working man. Gloria hates the violence between Bill and her son, but she takes comfort knowing that she can almost always diffuse the situation and stop Bill before he does something that "really" hurts Sammy.

Unfortunately, family members like Gloria often enable domestic violence to continue by taking the perpetrator "off the hook," so to speak. The violent behavior gets worse and everyone suffers. Friends and neighbors who hear or see the violence often try not to "notice" or give the victim advice about what they should or shouldn't do to avoid provoking the abuser. Even today, in many parts of the United States, law enforcement officials often hesitate to step in on domestic abuse situations, especially those between a husband and a wife.

Why do family members, friends, neighbors, or even the police assume the enabling role if it only makes things worse? Because they act out of misguided beliefs, feelings, and attitudes about family loyalty, protection, and privacy. These misguided beliefs, feelings, and attitudes cause them to see all that they do as sincere efforts to help the perpetrator and the family. Or, they may be afraid for their own safety or afraid of how the problems the perpetrator might cause if confronted could affect the family's reputation, stability, or income. Lacking the knowledge of what violence is (whenever anyone inflicts or threatens to inflict physical or emotional injury or discomfort upon another person's body, feelings, or possessions) and how violence can work to make the whole family system dysfunctional or even destroy the family, enablers continue to act out of misguided sympathy, loyalty, or fear of retribution by the perpetrator.

It can be just as hard for enablers to stop their enabling behavior as it is to get the perpetrators to stop their abusive behavior. Why? For one thing enabling often enhances the enabler's sense of strength or self-esteem or gives them a false sense of security, as reflected in the statements below:

- "I'll never tell what goes on here. The family can count on me."

- "We are a *close* family and we take care of our *own* problems."

- "It's no one's business what goes on in our home. We don't air our dirty laundry in public."

- "If I work harder in school and get good grades like Mom wants, she'll probably stop being so mad all the time."

With regard to violence problems in school, believing he or she is helping to keep violent kids out of trouble by protecting them and their families from the consequences of the kids' violent behavior can sometimes be a source of self-esteem for a teacher, administrator, or other school professional. When they believe they are doing good for the student and everyone else involved, it becomes easier and safer for enablers to ignore their own honest feelings or perceptions than to take the risk to talk openly about them. Moreover, an educator who fails to report a student who has threatened or actually used violence against himself or herself or another student or teacher may be doing so as a way of protecting his or her relationship with the student, of avoiding some kind of reaction by the student's parents, or retaliation by the student or the student's friends. By not reporting or confronting the student about his or her violent behavior, the educator also avoids facing his or her own feelings of fear or inadequacy. It is also possible that numbers of school professionals may feel uncomfortable reporting or confronting students about their violent behavior because of their own unresolved issues around violence problems in their own families.

Like families and individuals, feelings of self-esteem or false pride abide in *systems* as well. School systems often deny they have real violence problems because they want to protect their sense of worth as systems.

All attempts then, to change our individual enabling behaviors or those of a system require taking the double risk of self-examination and behavioral change. Until we are willing to take those risks we cannot make significant headway in solving violence problems in our schools.

Enabling as Unwitting and Unintentional

It cannot be stressed too strongly that enablers do not *cause* violence problems in schools, that they are not to be held responsible for or to *blame* for students' violent behaviors, and therefore they should not feel guilty. In fact, enabling is almost always instinctive, unwitting, and unintentional. Much of our enabling is unconscious; we act or react on the basis of misguided beliefs, feelings, and attitudes that often lie beneath our conscious awareness. Enabling is also unwitting in another sense. Even if we are conscious of our enabling behavior, we are typically not aware of its harmful effects. A classroom teacher who fails to report a student who has threatened or has actually been violent in the classroom because he or she didn't want to cause "trouble" for the student may not be aware that this decision contributes in an important way to the enabling system surrounding that student and many other students. No one consciously says, "I think I will help someone get away with violent behavior today."

In assisting individuals and systems to examine their enabling, it is vital to accept that *people do the best they can with what they know.* Enabling arises and acquires force because we act on inadequate or inaccurate information (misguided beliefs) and are unaware of the consequences of the feelings and attitudes that follow from such misguided beliefs. What is crucial is that we become *aware* of *enabling behaviors* in ourselves and in the system we belong to and that we *stop* those behaviors.

■ How Educators Act as Enablers

We have looked at how our misguided beliefs, feelings, attitudes, and behavior can unwittingly make us enablers—that is, can cause us to do or omit certain actions that prevent or shield those who act in violent ways from realizing and experiencing the consequences of their behavior. Now we need to examine more specifically:

1) How we can be unwitting enablers of violence problems in our individual roles within the school.

2) How we collectively—as classroom teachers, student services specialists, administrators, and other staff members—can unintentionally create a powerful enabling system in the school that actively encourages or allows violence problems to develop, continue, and worsen.

Role-Related Conduct of Individuals

Because students interact with educators (teachers, administrative staff, and other professionals within the school) in various ways depending on the educator's role, some kinds of enabling are more characteristic of certain educators than of others. Here are some ways in which classroom teachers, counselors, and administrators often enable. (For a comprehensive list of specific enabling patterns commonly observed or reported by educators themselves, see the "Professional Enabling Checklist" at the back of this booklet.)

Classroom Teachers

Teachers usually interact with students more often and more regularly than other educators do. In general, enabling by teachers most frequently involves failure to identify, report, and refer students who threaten to use or actually use violence in the classroom, in the hallways, or other observable areas in the school. Here are some common enabling behaviors of classroom teachers:

- Avoiding places in the school building or school grounds where students are known to act in aggressive or violent ways that may require intervention by a responsible adult.

- Failing to observe, confront, intervene with, or report threats of or actual violent interactions between students or between students and themselves in such areas as classrooms, hallways, lavatories, or cafeterias.

- Ignoring unacceptable or threatening behavior in the classroom.

- Ignoring reports of or complaints by other students who have been threatened or have actually been victims of violent behavior by other students.

- Ignoring students' verbal statements in class about planning to use violence against another student or a teacher, or about possessing a weapon.

- Refusing to openly express feelings of anger, sadness, fear, or concern when students brag or talk about their use of violence against people.

- Refusing to report rumors of planned fights on the school grounds or before or after school.

- Refusing to report rumors about students who may be carrying weapons in school.

- Having unclear or inconsistent standards of acceptable academic performance and classroom conduct.

- Failing to report incidents of violence or threats of violence to appropriate school authorities or to those designated to handle such incidents.

- Attempting to handle the threats of or actual violent actions of students by trying to counsel them oneself or by using abusive language or personal threats such as lowering grades or reporting to the principal.

- Maintaining preconceived notions (stereotypes and judgmental attitudes), such as "Only bad kids are responsible for violence problems," thereby often excusing violent behavior of "good kids" as understandable, necessary for self-defense, or simply not "as bad" as when the "bad kids" act in similar ways.

Student Service Specialists

School social workers, counselors, psychologists, and other student service specialists are traditionally in the most advantageous position to discover the nature and severity of students' problems, including use of or involvement in violent incidents at school or at home. While to some degree student service specialists are susceptible to the same enabling behaviors as other school professionals, some enabling is directly related to the screening and assessment functions these specialists are called to perform. The following are some common enabling behaviors that can hinder student service specialists from identifying, assessing, and effectively dealing with students involved in violence.

- Making judgments or decisions or taking action without formal training in violence prevention and intervention concepts and skills.

- Failing to include questions about use of violence or involvement in violent incidents at school, at home, or in the streets as a routine part of counseling sessions with troubled or problem students.

- Regarding certain kinds of violent behaviors among students as acceptable (rationalizing certain violent incidents, thereby condoning violence).

- Believing, prior to investigation, that a good student couldn't possibly have threatened to use violence or that the student doesn't have the capacity to perpetrate violence or carry a weapon.

- Attempting to deal with students' violent threats or actual behavior alone, without involving others on staff who may have special training or expertise for dealing with the student's specific issues or who may be specifically assigned to deal with problems of violent behavior.

- Failing to notify or involve appropriate school authorities in dealing with a violence prone student.

- Failing to follow proper protocol in dealing with a student referred for violent behavior or making threats.

- Failing to refer to appropriate community resources (for evaluation, counseling, or both) students who do not respond to school services.

Administrators

Principals and assistant principals become enablers primarily by virtue of their roles in developing and enforcing school policies (for example, administering corrective discipline or consequences for unacceptable behavior). Here are some specific ways in which they may enable violence:

- Taking action without formal training in violence prevention and intervention concepts and skills that are especially designed for schools.

- Taking disciplinary action with students involved in violent incidents without consulting or involving other school professionals, such as counselors, social workers, or Student Assistance Program coordinators.

- Attempting to use personal threats or punitive measures in private to dissuade students from using or threatening to use violence in the school.

- Taking disciplinary action without first attempting to find out more about the degree of severity or frequency of a student's use of violence or involvement in violent incidents.

- Taking disciplinary action merely to punish rather than provide students with the help or opportunity to change their behavior.

- Failing to take disciplinary action on perpetrators of violence for fear of parental or community reaction.

- Failing to openly admit and address violence problems in the school (thereby placing other educators and students at risk) in order to protect one's professional position or the school's image.

- Permitting certain traditional school activities, such as "freshman initiation rites," that involve put-downs, humiliations, and other forms of physical or emotional abuse of students.

- Blaming the violence problems in the school on parents, the police, the media, gangs, drug dealers, or others, while refusing to look at the school's contribution to such problems.

- Relying on ineffective, militant *responses* to violence problems in the schools (such as installing metal detectors, placing bars on windows, hiring armed security guards, requesting the help of police to "rid the school of the cause of violence—weapons and gangs," or installing cameras on buses) without developing and implementing school policies and procedures for dealing with all violent behavior.

- Implementing single-focus or piecemeal programs (such as anger management and conflict resolution skills training or peer mediation programs) as the "solution" to the complex and multifaceted problem of violence, without developing and implementing school policies and procedures for dealing with violent behavior.

- Failing to provide formal training for all staff and for parents on violence prevention and intervention concepts and skills.

- Developing and enforcing a militant or punitive "get tough" policy on violent behavior that focuses only on weapons and gangs and does not include provisions for systematically determining and addressing the frequency and severity of any individual student's involvement in violence (for example, through assessment, education, counseling, support, and referral).

Others in the School Setting

Similar lists can be devised for others in the school setting who work with or serve student needs in a special way. For instance, coaches and other athletic staff often contribute to the enabling system by:

- Failing to establish, adopt, or take seriously athletic codes and training rules that prohibit use of violence in sports competition.

- Failing to enforce consequences for violations or enforcing the consequences preferentially or only if such consequences would not affect a team's status, potential for winning, or a particular student's chances of obtaining an athletic scholarship.

- Covering up or excusing athletes' violations of the athletic code or training rules, or reducing penalties for violations by athletes.

- Allowing or encouraging violent behavior in games or practice as a means of "toughening up" players or increasing "aggressiveness" or the "will to win."

- Engaging in an attitude of "win at all costs" when coaching young people.

- Overlooking humiliating or abusive language or destructive activities, such as put downs, racial slurs, or derogatory comments about others' bodies or abilities.

The fact that athletes are often exempted from the "no-violence" rule or are not expected to confront one another for use of violence only contributes to how students themselves develop enabling behaviors. Also, in many cases, coaches and trainers are exempted from the no-violence rule and are unwilling to examine their own use of abusive or punitive language or behavior all in the name of "making boys into men"—or in terms more appropriate for the realities of today, "making children (girls and boys) into strong, competitive athletes."

At least two other groups, however, deserve formal mention in any discussion of enabling in the school setting: *students* and *parents*. Violence problems in students develop, persist, and worsen in part because of parental enabling (see the *Parent Enabling Checklist* at the back of this booklet). Parental enabling usually begins with the overwhelming need to protect both the student and the family from being criticized, judged, or condemned by outsiders and from the feelings of shame, guilt, or loss of self-respect that such criticism or judgment creates. Enabling by parents is usually even more emotionally intense than that of people outside the family, such as teachers or coaches. Denial and enabling are often especially pronounced in families in which physical, emotional, or sexual abuse (family violence) has produced anger and rage in a student who then turns that anger or rage against classmates or teachers. This often accounts for the resistance educators may encounter when they attempt to work with the parents of a student in trouble for violent behavior.

Finally, adolescents spend most of their time not with parents or teachers, but with one another in a well-defined peer culture with its own pattern of misguided beliefs, feelings, attitudes, and behaviors concerning the use of violence. As we try to change the enabling system in a school, we must ask how students themselves enable violence problems to develop, persist, and worsen (See the *Student Enabling Checklist*). And we must provide a way for students to become aware of these patterns and ways they can change them so that they will not feel so helpless to do something about the violence they claim to fear.

For example, a student's violent behavior is often rationalized and justified—by both students and adults—by saying the incident was a result of "peer pressure." We hear, "I had to fight him when he said that about me in front of those other guys," or "If I hadn't hit him they would think I was a wimp (or a punk or I would have looked stupid)." It is important to expose students to the concept of "enabling" when they complain of "peer pressure." This forces the responsibility for the choices students make about using violence back on themselves instead of on their peers. It also forces students to look at their own *tendencies* to support a friend's fighting as "enabling." In other words, students need to learn that if they hit someone it is because *they chose* to, not because someone else made them or encouraged them to do it.

One other aspect of enabling violence problems in schools that we need to ask ourselves about is how we might be enabling with respect to those students who are being *victimized by violence in their homes* (family or domestic violence). This is not to imply that educators are ever to be blamed for or held responsible for how children are affected by family violence. Through reluctance to become informed about or to talk openly about the effects of family violence on children, however, educators reinforce the "no-talk rule" or imposed silence that students learn at home. This serves to increase the guilt, shame, and sense of isolation these students feel.

Conduct of the System

It eventually becomes evident to responsible school professionals who are willing to look at their own individual enabling behaviors that their collective enabling patterns may have become institutionalized—that is, they may have become part of the school system itself. To understand this "enabling system," we ask the same general questions we asked individuals: How are various misguided beliefs, feelings, attitudes, and behaviors concerning violence reflected in our collective behavior?

Schools need to examine how enabling is reflected in at least three specific areas at the system level:

- Policies and Procedures

- Responsibility

- Support

Policies and Procedures

Clearly, not having formal policies and procedures governing incidents of violence in a school system is a sure way to keep that system helpless to handle such problems. Even if a school system has established such policies and procedures, however, the policies and procedures themselves can be a form of enabling if, among other failings:

- The policy does not clearly define what it means by violent behavior.

- The policy, though clearly and widely promoted, is generally not enforced, thus communicating a double message to everyone in the school system, but especially to students.

- The policy does not lay down clear and firm consequences for violations, including provisions for assessment and support for students to help them change their behavior.

- The policy is too narrow, focusing on or covering only certain aspects of violence, such as weapons, gangs, or physical assaults, but not the use of hurtful words, looks, signs, or gestures that often provoke physical assaults.

- The policy is so punitive in tone that students, teachers, and other school professionals, as well as parents are afraid, unwilling, or refuse to support it.

The absence of clearly defined procedures, or the assumption that the handling of violence problems is someone else's job, and should, or will be, handled by that someone, contributes highly to the school's inability to effectively deal with violence problems. In such circumstances, different students may be dealt with differently (or unequally) by different educators, or perhaps, not dealt with at all. Moreover, the absence of clearly defined procedures (including the steps for following through) often means that if a student is reported for violent behavior, no one is sure what to do, which options are available, what the next step should be, or who should be notified or involved—when, where, and how.

Responsibility

Students must be taught by responsible adults within the school that no one is entitled to use violence for any reason and that violence will not be tolerated. The key to preventing violence lies in shaping students' beliefs, feelings, attitudes, and behaviors *before* violence becomes an automatic tool for expressing anger, handling conflicts, or simply for getting what they need, want, or expect. This is actually achieved first by changing adults' misguided beliefs, feelings, attitudes, and behaviors concerning violence. The next step in preventing student violence is decisive, determined, and consistent action on the part of adult educators who have collectively agreed to act to prevent or intervene with any student who threatens or uses violence and to follow the school's policy and procedures for reporting and following through on the incident.

Any policy (and its procedures) governing incidents of violence that is worthwhile must be based on a centralized team approach that includes a centralized and systematic reporting system. By using a centralized team approach (core team or committee) with a centralized and systematic reporting system, schools have an efficient tool for sorting out and dealing appropriately, fairly, and effectively with different students engaged in different levels of violence at different times. Such an approach would necessarily include a systematic and structured intervention process that helps determine over time the degree, frequency, and severity of a student's involvement with violence. When patterns of violent behavior are identified, the students can then be offered the level of help and support they need. Of course the core team or committee, along with all school staff, need to be trained to deal with violence issues and problems in order for them to act effectively and responsibly.

Support

When we examine our school systems for enabling in the areas of policies and procedures and responsibility, we also need to examine it in the area of support given or withheld.

Fragmented effort is the opposite of support and mutually assured responsibility—the guarantee that if one staff member takes step A, the others will take steps B and C. Classroom teachers and other school professionals must feel confident that if they take the risk to refer a student for violent behavior, the core team or committee will follow through according to school policy and procedures. And the core team or committee must be assured that if they need administrative support, it is unequivocally available. Administrators need to be able to trust that core team or committee members or counselors, or other school staff, won't act to get certain students off the hook by protecting them from the consequences of their behavior. Finally, the staff and administration need to know that the board of education and the community support the firm enforcement of a school policy that couples choices and consequences with help and support.

What Can be Done About Enabling?

Any effective response to violence problems in schools requires stopping the enabling behaviors that result in *entitlement* and *tolerance*. Again, Johnson Institute research shows that it is these two pervasive attitudes that are fueling the escalation of violence problems in schools. Entitlement to and tolerance of violence in school cannot exist for long when enabling stops.

The first step in stopping enabling is to educate the enablers themselves about the concept of enabling, especially with regard to violence problems. Often, much of the enabling is eliminated as soon as those involved have a framework for examining their own behavior. Since enabling is unwitting and unintentional, it has to be made *conscious*. Each of the factors mentioned earlier has to be exposed: misguided beliefs, feelings, attitudes, and behaviors concerning violence. Education for all school personnel is necessary— including intensive training for developing anger management and conflict resolution skills, skills for safe intervention with students and for self-protection—if they are to act collectively, consistently, knowledgeably, and effectively in solving violence problems.

The second step is to give school personnel the opportunity to examine the deeper sources of enabling in themselves and to discuss them in a safe environment where no blaming or judgment occurs. Educators at all levels must learn to confront enabling in themselves as well as in others.

The third step is that the school system has to allow

its staff members to deal openly and safely with their own personal experiences with violence problems. For example, staff members who are themselves victims of family violence (or were as children) or who are themselves perpetrators of violence in their own families may not be able to respond to violence problems in students in healthy ways. Clearly, how effective we are at creating an environment that discourages enabling will depend on how willing we are to admit to and deal with violence problems in ourselves.

Finally, there must be commitment, leadership, and support for change, as well as a supportive atmosphere. In large part, changing one's enabling behavior almost always entails risk—to one's sense of well-being and personal safety, to one's relationships with students and parents, and sometimes to one's position. It is difficult to adopt new ways of dealing with violence problems unless others support the changes. There is a positive note to be sounded regarding most people's willingness today to do something about violence in our schools. It is very clear that many schools do report violence problems, and that both staff and the vast majority of students in those schools are highly motivated to do something about the problem. Unlike other problems, such as alcohol or other drug abuse, where staff, students, and parents are more reluctant to acknowledge the problem, deal openly with it, or cooperate in a school's efforts to do something about it, the problem of violence is so pervasive and has created such fear that few feel indifferent to it.

Students are waiting for adults to become responsible and to change the school environment. Most educators are afraid of violence problems, too, and want to do something about them. They need to be shown how much power they do have to transform a violence-prone school system into a safe, supportive, nurturing, and nonpunitive learning atmosphere where both adults and children feel protected and respected. They simply need a comprehensive plan and strategy to do it. The first step in that plan is to address the enabling factor.

Conclusion

The approach to enabling presented in this booklet stresses the interaction between students who use violence and a school system that unwittingly and unintentionally encourages or allows violence problems to develop, continue, and worsen. The positive message of this booklet is that the entire school system and the individuals within that system *can* solve violence problems if they become *aware* of the concept of enabling, consciously examine how enabling manifests itself within the school system, and courageously set about making the required changes.

Many schools have already attempted to implement various violence-prevention strategies, but with little long-term success. The Johnson Institute maintains that where prevention in any form has failed, the reason almost always has to do with some form of enabling or the failure to address it. A peer mediation program aimed at preventing or alleviating student violence problems will have limited success if the students and staff do not understand that there can be a fine line between "helping" and "enabling." Moreover, use of peer mediation for dealing with bully/victim types of conflict is ineffective and inappropriate and can be a form of enabling itself, because it is based on a misguided belief that all forms of student violence are the same.

The most effective curriculum for building self-esteem in students will be ineffective as a means of preventing violence if students live or participate in a school system or environment that allows violence problems to continue unchecked. Teaching students about decision making as a measure for preventing violence is useless unless students are helped to make responsible decisions by experiencing the consequences of those *irresponsible* decisions they have already made.

Finally, teaching anger management and conflict resolution skills is fruitless without a strong school ethos that is collectively and unequivocally supported and articulated by all adults in the school:

> *No one is* ENTITLED *to use violence in this school.*

> *We* DO NOT TOLERATE *it here.*

To the extent that individuals and systems become fully aware of themselves, they will know how to change. Prevention of violence problems must begin by examining and changing those misguided beliefs, feelings, attitudes, and behaviors that unwittingly allow or encourage violence to develop and persist.

Appendix
Enabling Checklists*

The checklists that follow give many specific examples of the misguided beliefs, feelings, attitudes, and behaviors concerning violence that make up the enabling system. The *School Professionals Checklist*, although longer than the others, is still not exhaustive. It can be used as an informal self-test to help district administrators, teachers, counselors, coaches, student service specialists, and other school staff to identify patterns of enabling in themselves or others. It can be used in its entirety or items can be selected for use with specific groups

The *Parent Enabling Checklist* focuses on some additional enabling factors that apply especially to parents. It can be useful for parent training sessions, workshops, seminars, support groups, and so on. The checklist will be useful to schools for helping parents identify how they might be enabling their children's use of or involvement in violence problems.

The *Student Enabling Checklist* can be useful to teachers and counselors as they deal with students who use or are involved in violence. It is an ideal tool to use in student support groups for both perpetrators and victims of violence.

• The Enabling Checklists for School Professionals, Parents, and Students are adapted from those appearing in *Enabling in the School Setting* by Gary Anderson (Minneapolis: Johnson Institute, 1988), and are used here with permission of the author

School Professionals Checklist

Indicate the degree to which each statement applies to you.

Yes	No	Sometimes	
☐	☑	☐	1. I overlook obvious problems in students who use violence or who are involved in violent situations.
☐	☑	☐ ← eye roller	2. I oversimplify problem behaviors in students who use violence.
☐	☐	☐	3. I make decisions or take actions even though I lack formal training in violence prevention and intervention concepts and strategies.
☐	☐	☐	4. I view violent behavior in students as primarily a moral issue.
☐	☐	☐	5. In the staff lounge, I gossip about the violent behavior of students.
☐	☐	☐	6. When I talk about students who are bullying others or who have problems controlling their anger, my tone is accusatory.
☐	☐	☐	7. I view students who bully others or who have trouble resolving conflicts nonviolently as "bad kids."
☐	☐	☐	8. I feel angry, tense, or anxious about having to deal with violence problems in school.
☐	☐	☐	9. I place the blame for the increase in students' violent behavior somewhere other than on the students themselves.

Yes	No	Sometimes	
☐	☐	☐	10. I lack clear, definite standards of performance and conduct for students while in school.
☐	☐	☐	11. I've gradually lowered my expectations for acceptable student performance in my classroom.
☐	☐	☐	12. I'm uncomfortable bringing up the subject of bullying or use of violence when I'm working with troubled students.
☐	☐	☐	13. When I see a student using violence against another person I avoid the problem.
☐	☐	☐	14. When I see acts of violence among students, I don't report it.
☐	☐	☐	15. I take disciplinary action with violent students without consulting the appropriate professionals in the school.
☐	☐	☐	16. I hesitate to involve others when dealing with violent students because I fear that the students or the situation will be mishandled.
☐	☐	☐	17. I hesitate to take action with violent students because I fear the school district will not support me.
☐	☐	☐	18. I don't take action with students who are bullying others because I'm afraid the victim will be mistreated again.
☐	☐	☐	19. I'm afraid of parental or community reactions if I take action on a student's violent behavior.
☐	☐	☐	20. I set a healthy example for students through the way I handle conflicts nonviolently.

Yes	No	Sometimes	
☐	☐	☐	21. I've used violent language or actions while dealing with students.
☐	☐	☐	22. I wait for students' violent behavior problems to change by themselves.
☐	☐	☐	23. I protect students from experiencing consequences by minimizing the seriousness of their violent behavior.
☐	☐	☐	24. I fail to admit the extent of violence problems to protect the school's image.
☐	☐	☐	25. I feel violence problems in the school should be handled by the administration.
☐	☐	☐	26. I hesitate to confront students' use of violence for fear of jeopardizing my relationship with them.
☐	☐	☐	27. I feel some behaviors described as violent are just normal behavior for children and adolescents.
☐	☐	☐	28. As long as no one is being physically hurt, I look the other way when I see students name-calling, teasing, using put-downs, or provoking others.
☐	☐	☐	29. I believe the violence problems in our school would stop if we could get rid of the bad kids who cause it.
☐	☐	☐	30. I believe that the students I work with are "above" bullying others or using violence in other ways.
☐	☐	☐	31. I avoid confronting students who are bullying others or involved in other acts of violence because I am afraid for my own safety.

Yes	No	Sometimes	
☐	☐	☐	32. When students disclose that they are victims of violence at home I fear the consequences of taking action.
☐	☐	☐	33. Discussions of, or involvement with violence prevention and intervention problems are "too close to home" for me.
☐	☐	☐	34. I regard a certain degree of student bullying or other acts of violence as unavoidable and therefore acceptable.
☐	☐	☐	35. I make excuses for, cover up, and even defend certain students involved in bullying or other acts of violence.
☐	☐	☐	36. I become frustrated at my inability to change a student's violent behavior.
☐	☐	☐	37. I feel inadequate and guilty when I fail to take action with students' violent behavior.
☐	☐	☐	38. I maintain a "no-talk rule" concerning students who use violence or students who are victims of violence.
☐	☐	☐	39. I avoid places in the building where I know violent students tend to bully others or where they tend to go to fight.
☐	☐	☐	40. I do not believe the school should be involved in solving students' problems related to violence.
☐	☐	☐	41. I have ignored the violent or bullying behaviors of staff.
☐	☐	☐	42. I have allowed students to avoid the consequences of their violent behavior to protect their academic or athletic status.

Yes	No	Sometimes	
☐	☐	☐	43. I believe that the best thing to teach students who are victims of violence by other students is to fight back.
☐	☐	☐	44. I believe the best medicine for bullies is to have stronger, older students give them a taste of their own medicine.

Parent Enabling Checklist

The statements below describe certain misguided beliefs, feelings, attitudes, and behaviors concerning violence that can be a part of a complex enabling system. Johnson Institute defines violent behavior as occurring *whenever anyone inflicts or threatens to inflict physical or emotional injury or discomfort upon another person's body, feelings, or possessions.* Indicate the degree to which each statement applied to your experience with a child who may have a problem with violent behavior.

Yes No Sometimes

☐ ☐ ☐ 1. My child has threatened me with violence, but I have been afraid to say anything to my spouse or another adult.

☐ ☐ ☐ 2. I have avoided talking to anyone at school or to a counseling agency about my child's violent behavior out of fear of the stigma.

☐ ☐ ☐ 3. I no longer trust my child's ability to control his or her anger and aggression.

☐ ☐ ☐ 4. I doubt my own perceptions about my child's violent behavior. I think I may be making something out of nothing.

☐ ☐ ☐ 5. I blame myself for my child's violent behavior; if I'd been a better parent, I could have prevented this.

☐ ☐ ☐ 6. I feel inadequate as a parent.

☐ ☐ ☐ 7. I increasingly feel angry and afraid of my child's violent behavior.

☐ ☐ ☐ 8. I am fearful or tense when my child is in a bad mood.

Yes	No	Sometimes	
☐	☐	☐	9. I don't think my child cares how I/we feel as parents about his or her violent behavior.
☐	☐	☐	10. I excuse my child's violent behavior by attributing it to adolescence (or another developmental stage)—he or she will "grow out of it."
☐	☐	☐	11. I have given up on expecting my child to follow family rules of conduct.
☐	☐	☐	12. I have justified my child's violence at home and at school because of the pressures he or she is under from bullies, drug dealers, kids who carry weapons, and gang members.
☐	☐	☐	13. I don't believe my child has a problem with violent behavior because he or she doesn't fit my image of people who do.
☐	☐	☐	14. I maintain a "no-talk rule" by not discussing with other family members painful events, feelings, or the possibility of a violent behavior problem in our family.
☐	☐	☐	15. I blame my child's violent behavior on the kids he or she hangs around with.
☐	☐	☐	16. I attempt to control my child's behavior by becoming more sympathetic and understanding.
☐	☐	☐	17. I focus blame for my child's violent behavior on the fact that the police and the school are not doing their jobs.
☐	☐	☐	18. I endure; I think my child will eventually stop being violent if I am patient.

Yes	No	Sometimes	
☐	☐	☐	19. My spouse (or other family members) and I disagree about how to handle my child's violent behavior problem.
☐	☐	☐	20. When my child complains of being bullied or harassed by other kids, I tell him or her to "ignore them" or to "stand up for him or herself and fight back."
☐	☐	☐	21. Other family members and I sometimes do chores that were formerly my child's responsibility rather than risk having him or her become violent.
☐	☐	☐	22. I prevent our child from experiencing the consequences of his or her violent behavior by "covering" for him/her when he/she gets into trouble with police, school, or others.
☐	☐	☐	23. I keep other family members from knowing of my concerns or of facts I have about my child's violent behavior outside our home.
☐	☐	☐	24. I protect other family members from knowing about other problem situations or incidents involving violent actions by my child.
☐	☐	☐	25. I and/or my spouse tolerate some violent language or physical threats by our child.
☐	☐	☐	26. I and/or my spouse are sometimes verbally and physically abusive to each other.
☐	☐	☐	27. Our child has seen me or my spouse when we were verbally or physically abusive with each other.

Yes	No	Sometimes	
☐	☐	☐	28. I sometimes lose control (hitting or slapping) when I've attempted to discipline my child.
☐	☐	☐	29. I have sometimes regretted the things I've said or the names I've called my child when disciplining him or her.
☐	☐	☐	30. Even though we have expectations at home, I have given up getting my child to follow them.
☐	☐	☐	31. I've given up trying to tell my child how I feel; he or she doesn't care.
☐	☐	☐	32. In order to avoid conflict with my child, I just let him or her do what he/she wants or go where he/she wants.
☐	☐	☐	33. My child's violent temper tantrums are caused by the situation at school. If his or her teacher were more understanding, he or she wouldn't get so upset.

Student Enabling Checklist

Each statement below describes a misguided belief, feeling, attitude, or behavior concerning violence that can be a part of a complex enabling system. Johnson Institute defines violence as *any mean word, look, sign, or act that hurts a person's body, feelings, or things*. Indicate the degree to which each statement applies to your own experience with other students or your family members.

Yes No Sometimes

☐ ☐ ☐   1. I don't believe that students should report other students for violent behavior.

☐ ☐ ☐   2. I have stood by and watched while other students were involved in a violent argument or fight without saying or doing anything to stop it.

☐ ☐ ☐   3. I would rather that another student kept on being violent than report him or her to a school counselor or teacher.

☐ ☐ ☐   4. I have been concerned about a friend's or another student's violent behavior, but have been afraid to talk to him or her about it.

☐ ☐ ☐   5. I have been concerned about a friend's or another student's violent behavior, but have not talked to a school counselor or teacher about it.

☐ ☐ ☐   6. I am afraid if I share my concerns about a friend's or another student's violent behavior, I will lose his or her friendship.

Yes	No	Sometimes	
☐	☐	☐	7. I am afraid that if I share my concern about a friend's or another student's violent behavior with a counselor or teacher, it would ruin my reputation at school.
☐	☐	☐	8. I blame other people or circumstances for a friend's or another student's violent behavior problems.
☐	☐	☐	9. I have threatened to use or actually have used violence myself to get what I needed or wanted from another student or adult.
☐	☐	☐	10. I have protected, covered up, or lied about a friend's or another student's violent behavior problems so he or she wouldn't get into trouble.
☐	☐	☐	11. I have seen certain students bully weaker or younger students, but did nothing to stop it.
☐	☐	☐	12. I don't tell school authorities about violent incidents I know about.
☐	☐	☐	13. I have witnessed certain students bullying other students who couldn't defend themselves, but did not try to report it to school authorities.
☐	☐	☐	14. I have encouraged friends or other students to fight back when someone calls them names, puts them down, or provokes them in some way.
☐	☐	☐	15. I have known beforehand that a certain student was going to be beaten up after school, but did not report it to a school counselor or teacher.

Yes	No	Sometimes	
☐	☐	☐	16. I believe the only way to fight violence is with more violence.
☐	☐	☐	17. If anyone in my family used violence against another family member, I would not tell anyone about it.
☐	☐	☐	18. I believe problems with violence in my home should be handled by my family and no one else.
☐	☐	☐	19. I believe that if I or another student is challenged to fight, we have to fight or we'll look stupid or look like wimps.
☐	☐	☐	20. If another student uses violence against a brother, a sister, or a friend, I feel it is my responsibility to get revenge.
☐	☐	☐	21. I have participated in teasing students who everybody else picks on.
☐	☐	☐	22. I would not feel comfortable talking with other kids about how I feel about bullying.
☐	☐	☐	23. To me, violence is just a way of life. In our school, it's "fight or get stomped on."

Reference Notes

1. "Survey Finds School Violence Hits One in Four Students." *The New York Times*, December 17, 1993, p. A37. Summarized in *Sunburst Update*, Winter 1994, pp. 1-2.

2. "Violence in Rural America: Looking Beyond the View from the Highway." *Midwest Forum Newsletter*, March 1993: Vol. 3., No. 1, p. 4.

3. Wheeler, E.D., and S.A. Baron. (1994) *Violence in our Schools, Hospitals and Public Places: A Prevention and Management Guide.* Ventura, Calif.: Pathfinder Publishing of California, p. 25.

4. Prothrow-Stith, D, and M. Weissman. (1991, 1993) *Deadly Consequences: How Violence is Destroying Our Teenage Population and a Plan to Begin Solving the Problem.*: New York: HarperPerennial, p. 175.

5. Olweus, D. *Bullying at School: What We Know and What We Can Do.* Cambridge, Mass.: Blackwell Publishers, 1993, p. 20.

6. Based on Olweus, D., 1993, pp. 21-48.

7. Olweus, D., 1993, p. 21.

8. Olweus, D., 1993, p. 102.